Ezra Pound in His Time and Beyond

The Influence of Ezra Pound on Twentieth-Century Poetry

Ezra Pound
1885–1972

Ezra Pound in His Time and Beyond

The Influence of Ezra Pound on Twentieth-Century Poetry

A Catalog of an Exhibition
Special Collections Department
Hugh M. Morris Library
by Jesse Rossa

February 14, 2006–June 13, 2006

University of Delaware Library
Newark, Delaware
2006

About the Cover

Drawing of Ezra Pound by Henri Gaudier-Brzeska. Pound used
this iconic image as the letterhead for his stationery.
Gaudier-Brzeska (1891–1915) was a French artist whose images
of Pound, especially this drawing and the sculpture "Hieratic
Head of Ezra Pound," are potent renderings of Pound's forceful
presence.

About the Frontispiece

A drawing of Ezra Pound by Wyndham Lewis originally printed
in the *Dial*, Volume LXIX, no. 3, September 1920.

All photographs are of materials from
Special Collections, University of Delaware Library.

ISBN 0-9712360-2-X

Copies of this publication may be obtained from:
    Office of the Director
    University of Delaware Library
    Newark, DE 19717-5267
    302-831-2231 phone
    302-831-1046 fax

An online version of "Ezra Pound in His Time and Beyond:
The Influence of Ezra Pound on Twentieth-Century Poetry"
may be found at www.lib.udel.edu/ud/spec.

The University of Delaware Library gratefully acknowledges
the generous assistance of the University of Delaware Library
Associates and the Melva B. Guthrie Endowment for their
support of this publication.

Printed by Graphic Communications Center, University of Delaware.

Contents

List of Illustrations

Acknowledgments

The University of Delaware Library is known throughout the scholarly world for its remarkable literary collections, with strengths ranging from the seventeenth century to the present. With the exhibition "Ezra Pound in His Time and Beyond: the Influence of Ezra Pound on Twentieth-Century Poetry," Special Collections showcases the rich collections of the University of Delaware Library in literary modernism.

The modernist movement which emerged in Europe in the first years of the twentieth century represented a self-conscious break with traditional forms and subject matter and brought a search for a distinctly contemporary mode of expression in all areas of the arts. Perhaps the most important literary figure in the early years of modernism was the expatriate American writer Ezra Pound. As a poet, critic, supporter, and indefatigable promoter of the modernist cause, Ezra Pound stands out more than any other individual of the twentieth century as responsible for the profound transformation which literature underwent in the early decades of that century. Because of his controversial political views, Pound continues to attract almost as much condemnation as he does accolades. Nevertheless, it is impossible to ignore the vital role he played in the modernist revolution. "Ezra Pound in His Time and Beyond" provides an in-depth examination of his place and influence in twentieth-century literature.

Exhibitions such as this could not take place without the creativity, hard work, and support of numerous individuals. In 2004 the University of Delaware Library acquired the comprehensive and renowned Ezra Pound Collection formed over decades by Robert A.Wilson. It is this Collection which serves as the centerpiece for "Ezra Pound In His Time and Beyond." I wish to acknowledge the loving care and dedication of this eminent bibliophile in the building of so notable a collection and I thank him for designating the University of Delaware Library as its home.

I wish to thank the Unidel Foundation whose support enabled the University of Delaware Library to acquire the Robert A.Wilson Ezra Pound Collection.

The University of Delaware Library Associates under the leadership of President Wilson J.C. Braun, Jr., who is himself a devoted bibliophile, has continued to provide generous assistance to the University of Delaware Library. I wish to thank all members of the University of Delaware Library Associates whose support is gratefully acknowledged.

I wish to thank David Roselle, President of the University of Delaware, and Daniel Rich, Provost, whose support for building library special collections of distinction is noteworthy. Their vision and commitment to acquiring such superb collections and primary resources are acknowledged with appreciation and admiration.

I wish to acknowledge the outstanding scholarship and creativity of Jesse Rossa, Assistant Librarian in Special Collections, who served as curator of the exhibition and is the author of this publication. His work was enhanced by the excellent leadership of Timothy Murray, Head of Special Collections, and Craig Wilson, Assistant Director for Library Collections.

I wish to acknowledge the assistance of the Melva B. Guthrie Endowment Fund for its support of this publication.

All of the above are thanked for their contributions to the collections and programs of the University of Delaware Library.

Susan Brynteson
The May Morris Director of Libraries
University of Delaware

Preface

The Special Collections Department of the University of Delaware
Library houses a magnificent collection of twentieth-century
literature focusing on American, British, and Irish literary
figures. Few literary figures of the twentieth century have
exerted such a profound influence on major writers of his time
and on succeeding generations of writers as has Ezra Pound.

A list of those writers who were the recipients of Pound's support
reads like a veritable "who's who" of twentieth-century literature
in English, as the current exhibition and accompanying
publication make abundantly clear. It is a tribute to the strength
of the literary collections in Special Collections that the works
of so many important writers can be brought together in one
exhibition.

Developing and maintaining connections with writers, book-
sellers, and collectors is a major factor in creating collections of
distinction. One collector who is also a writer and former bookseller, and with whom the Library has maintained close contact
over the years, is Robert A. Wilson, whose outstanding collection
on Ezra Pound is a recent addition to the collections in Special
Collections and which forms the basis for the current exhibition.

It is my pleasure to introduce the reader to a fascinating exhibition
with the sincere hope that all will not only read this publication
but also visit the exhibition itself. I promise you a rare treat.

David P. Roselle
President
University of Delaware

On Special Collections

As research libraries utilize more and more electronic resources, databases and electronic tools, and as access to digitized materials increases in the years to come, the holdings of libraries will become increasingly similar. What will remain to signify the distinctive identity of each research library will be the richness, strength, and depth of its Special Collections.

Access to collections of distinction is a major and enduring contribution of research libraries. Special collections provide the primary source material for future research and scholarship.

The Robert A.Wilson Collection is one of the finest Ezra Pound collections in existence. Its remarkable contents range from rare magazines and pamphlets to unique copies of materials with associations to important figures in the world of literature and the arts. The collection includes books and other materials that are seldom available to the research community, for example the first two books of Ezra Pound, neither of which has come on the market in over twenty years. Surely the Robert A.Wilson Ezra Pound Collection will be extensively used by scholars, now and in the future.

The University of Delaware is honored to be the home of this distinguished collection, now so handsomely and effectively exhibited and described in this publication, and proud to be one of the premier repositories for twentieth-century literature in the world.

Daniel Rich
Provost
University of Delaware

Prolegomenon

When the American poet Donald Hall interviewed Ezra Pound
for *The Paris Review*'s "Writers at Work" series in 1960,
Pound said, in response to Hall's mention that the sculptor
Henry Moore had found solace in Pound's book on the French
sculptor Henri Gaudier-Brzeska, "There is no doubt—that I have
been some use—to some people." At seventy-five years of age,
Pound's acknowledgment of his influence may have belied some
lingering doubts he may have had about his generosity, but those
who benefited from it changed the course of literature and the
arts in the twentieth century, and Pound played a key role in
promoting and helping other artists and writers. Pound's
bibliographer Donald Gallup has written that Pound "attempted
to give the 'movement' more of a focus, perhaps, than it ever
actually had, but by sheer force of personality and conviction he
effected a revolution which still, a half century later, seems
miraculous." It is the purpose of this exhibition to show the role
Pound played in the development of "the movement," as Gallup
termed it, of literary modernism, and in doing so shine a light on
a thread that wends its way through sixty years of literature in a
century in which literature changed dramatically.

Ernest Hemingway, in *A Moveable Feast*, said of Pound: "Ezra
was the most generous writer I have ever known and the most
disinterested. He helped poets, painters, sculptors and prose
writers that he believed in and he would help anyone whether he
believed in them or not if they were in trouble." Wyndham Lewis
said similarly, "In his attitude towards other peoples' work
Pound has been superlatively generous . . . He does not in the
least mind being in service to somebody (as do other people it is
usually found) if they have great talent." Even a brief perusal of

1

the names of the writers Pound championed, from James Joyce
and T.S. Eliot to Marianne Moore and Robert Frost, from
William Carlos Williams and H.D. (both classmates of Pound's
at the University of Pennsylvania) to Wyndham Lewis and
Charles Olson, show Pound's wide-ranging taste and interests.
The anthologies he compiled and magazines he edited (such as
Des Imagistes, *Active Anthology*, *BLAST*, and the *Exile*) all
served to further the cause of modernism, and his translations
from the Provençal, Italian, and ancient Chinese were
tremendously influential. In the early days of modernism—a
movement he himself spearheaded—Pound was the impresario,
seemingly everywhere, promoting writers, editing and
publishing, writing his own poems, reviews, and essays, and
serving as a guiding light and beacon. Although his years in
London and Paris (1910-1923) were the most productive, he
remained an important force afterwards, and when he was
hospitalized at St. Elizabeths Hospital in Washington, D.C.,
after World War II, many young writers made the pilgrimage
to visit him, such as Robert Lowell and Elizabeth Bishop. Upon
his return to Italy in 1958, he continued to publish sections
from his ongoing opus, the *Cantos*, and continued to receive
young visitors, such as the poet Allen Ginsberg, whose own
Beat Generation had been influenced by the modernist writers
thirty years earlier.

The University of Delaware Library is pleased to be able to
draw upon the recently acquired Ezra Pound Collection of
Robert A.Wilson, noted bookseller, author, publisher, and
bibliographer, for this exhibition. Wilson was able, over the
course of forty years, to compile a premier collection of books,
manuscripts, and other Pound ephemera, and many of the
materials displayed are a tribute to his discerning collecting eye.

By focusing this exhibition on Pound, it is possible to draw
on multiple other collections within the University of Delaware
Library Special Collections, such as the Louis Henry Cohn
Hemingway Collection, the Florence Reynolds/Jane Heap
collection, the *Pagany* archives, and strong holdings in Irish
literature, twentieth-century poetry, modernism, and little
magazines.

The exhibition and its accompanying catalog are organized
somewhat chronologically, as Pound's life and career warrant.
The exhibition intertwines the work of other writers as Pound
influenced and supported them, and also displays Pound's own
work. Brief explanatory notes for each section are included,
followed by a list of the works displayed.

This exhibition and catalog owe much to many people, and for
their advice and discussions regarding both aspects of Pound
and of exhibition design, I am indebted to Virginia Bartow,
Gerald Cloud, Sarah Funke, Shauna Hannibal, Barbara Heritage,
Sunil Iyengar, Henry Lyman, Christine Nelson, Raymond Nichols,
Michael Peich, Michael Russem, Mark Samuels Lasner, and
Barbara Stein.

Jesse Rossa
Assistant Librarian and
Curator of the Exhibition
Special Collections Department

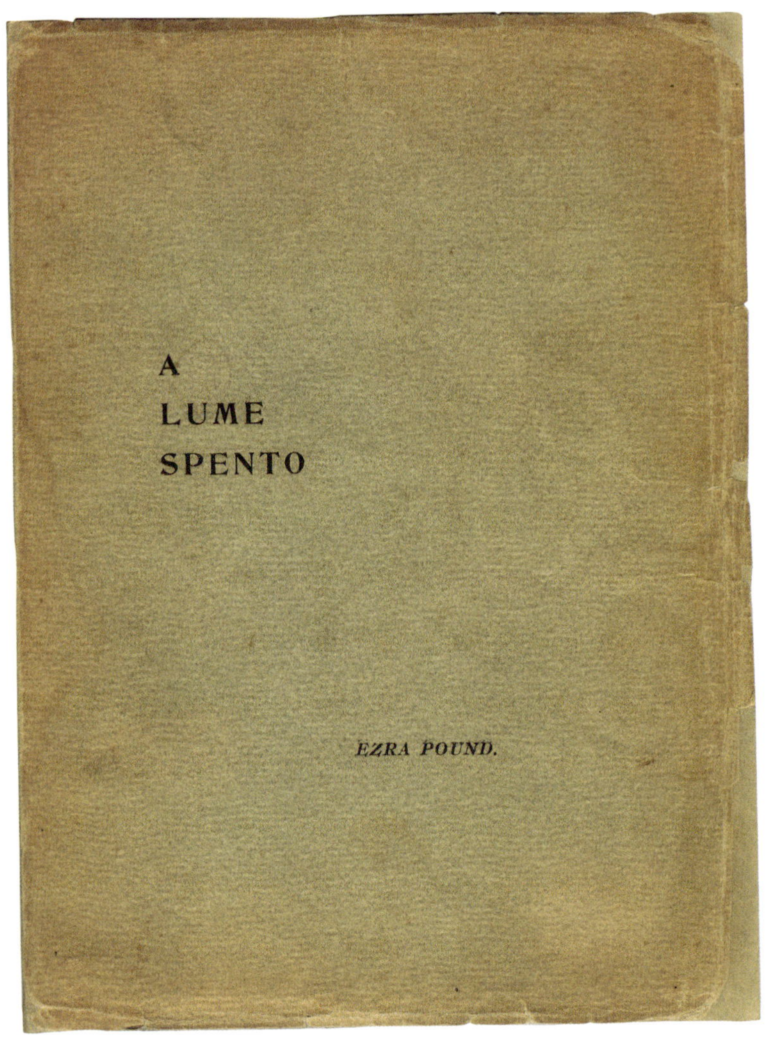

Ezra Pound. *A Lume Spento*. Venice: A. Antonini, 1908.

Ezra Pound in His Time and Beyond
The Influence of Ezra Pound on Twentieth-Century Poetry

Pound's Own Influences and Forebears

Ezra Pound's early work, culminating in the publication of
his first book, *A Lume Spento*, was infused with the spirit of the
Pre-Raphaelites, of Romanticism, of William Butler Yeats's
Celtic nocturnes, and especially of Robert Browning, particularly
Browning's penchant for dramatic monologues, assuming the
roles of different personae. Several years later, Browning's
Sordello served as a model for the narrative vision and scope of
the *Cantos*.

The young Pound was also very influenced by the Pre-Raphaelite
writer Algernon Charles Swinburne, whom he claimed kept alive
the notion of poetry as pure art, and whose rhythm and sound—
both extremely important elements in Pound's concept of poetry—
he admired greatly. "Swinburne beats us all," he wrote to
Archibald MacLeish in 1926.

Henry James was another influence, less for his style than as
an example of an American abroad in Europe (although Pound
later described his long poem *Hugh Selwyn Mauberley* as a
"Henry James novel in verse"). Pound wrote an extended
commentary on James's work after his death in 1916, which he
called a "Baedeker to a continent."

———

Robert Browning. *Dramatis Personae*. London: Chapman & Hall, 1864.
Robert Browning. *Sordello*. London: Edward Moxon, 1840.

Algernon Charles Swinburne. *Songs Before Sunrise*. London:
    F.S. Ellis, 1871.
Henry James. *Transatlantic Sketches*. Boston: J.R. Osgood, 1875.
Ezra Pound. *A Lume Spento*. Venice: A. Antonini, 1908.
Ezra Pound. *A Quinzaine for this Yule*. London: Pollack, 1908.
Ezra Pound. *Personae*. London: Elkin Mathews, 1909.

William Carlos Williams and H.D.: The Penn Years

Ezra Pound entered the University of Pennsylvania as a freshman
in 1901, at the age of fifteen. He transferred to Hamilton College
two years later, due to poor grades, and received his bachelor's
degree there in 1905. He returned to Penn later that year for
graduate work in Romance languages and literatures, and earned
his master's degree, but left before finishing his doctoral work.
(Before sailing for Venice in 1908, he had a brief stint as an
instructor at Wabash College in Crawfordsville, Indiana.)

While at Penn, he met a fellow student two years his senior who,
despite his pursuit of a degree in medicine, was also writing
poetry. William Carlos Williams and Pound became friends,
united by their poetic ambitions. Later, in London, Pound
persuaded Elkin Mathews to publish an early collection of
Williams's, *The Tempers*, and he reviewed it himself in the
New Freewoman ("He makes a bold attempt to express himself
directly and convinces one that the emotions expressed are
veritably his own. . ."). They did not always see eye to eye
regarding one another's work and lives—Pound sometimes found
Williams's work parochial, and Williams wrote with sadness and
anger in 1945 about Pound's cruel letters and anti-Semitism
(although he defended Pound as a poet)—still, their friendship,

6

with its ups and downs, lasted for decades. Williams's *Paterson* is often regarded, along with the *Cantos*, as one of the greatest long poems of the century.

In his freshman year at Penn, Pound became involved with Hilda Doolittle, the daughter of an astronomy professor. They courted for several years and had an unofficial, sporadic engagement, and he wrote a series of sonnets for her which he bound together as "Hilda's Book." In London in 1912, he was soon arranging to have her poetry published in *Poetry* magazine as "H.D.," the name under which she would publish for the next fifty years. One of her last works, written in 1958, was a memoir of Pound, *End to Torment.* "Torment title excellent, but optimistic," Pound replied when she sent him the manuscript for his comments.

——

William Carlos Williams. *The Tempers*. London: Elkin Mathews, 1913.

William Carlos Williams. *A Book of Poems, Al Que Quiere!* Boston: The Four Seas Company, 1917.

William Carlos Williams. *Kora in Hell: Improvisations*. Boston: The Four Seas Company, 1920.

William Carlos Williams. *Paterson*. New York: New Directions, 1946–58.

H.D. *Sea Garden*. London: Constable, 1916.

H.D. *Hymen*. New York: H. Holt and Company, 1921.

H.D. *End to Torment*. New York: New Directions, 1979.

Ezra Pound. *Exultations*. London: Elkin Mathews, 1909.

Ezra Pound. Autograph Document Signed, Contract with Elkin Mathews for *Exultations*, September 16, [1909].

Ezra Pound. *Provença*. Boston: Small, Maynard, 1910.

Ezra Pound. *Canzoni*. London: Elkin Mathews, 1911.

London: William Butler Yeats, Wyndham Lewis, and Others

Upon Pound's arrival in London in August 1908, he rapidly
insinuated himself into the city's literary scene, meeting, among
many others, the publisher Elkin Mathews (who was to publish
several of Pound's books, beginning with *Personae* in 1909),
Ford Madox Hueffer (later Ford Madox Ford), Olivia Shakespear
(W.B. Yeats' former lover, whose daughter, Dorothy, Pound
married in 1914), D.H. Lawrence, James Joyce, Robert Frost,
Wyndham Lewis, and perhaps most important of all,
William Butler Yeats.

Pound once said that Yeats was the original impetus for his move
to London; he wanted "to sit at Yeats' feet, and learn what he
knew." By 1908, Yeats was a major figure in poetry, and Pound,
like many other younger poets of the time, was deeply influenced
by him. Pound quickly met Yeats, and by 1913 was spending the
winters with him at Yeats's Stone Cottage in Sussex, acting as
his secretary. Pound played an active role in encouraging Yeats
to continue moving towards an elliptical, more colloquial style,
less influenced by Celtic mythology, which is seen in the poems
published in *Responsibilities* (1914) and *The Wild Swans at
Coole* (1917), and Pound admired the antiquarian leanings of
Yeats in turn. The writings of both men were very dissimilar
from one another; Yeats later said in *A Packet for Ezra Pound*,
"Ezra Pound, whose art is the opposite of mine, whose criticism
commends what I most condemn, a man with whom I should
quarrel more than with anyone else if we were not united by
affection."

Pound met Wyndham Lewis not long after his arrival in London,
but the two men did not see much of each other for several years,

BLAST.
Volume I, no.1, 1914.

and it was not until 1914 that they joined forces to publish the
journal *BLAST*, the manifesto of the Vorticist movement (an art
movement influenced by the Italian Futurists and the Cubists,
and named and described by Pound). Lewis was a painter and
writer; Pound was active in arranging for the serial publication
of his first novel, *Tarr*, in 1915. Although *BLAST* was only
published for two issues, its stark and aggressive design was
enormously influential.

———

William Butler Yeats. *Responsibilities*. New York: The Macmillan Co., 1916.
William Butler Yeats. *The Wild Swans at Coole*. Churchtown, Dundrum:
    The Cuala Press, 1917.
William Butler Yeats. *A Packet for Ezra Pound*. Dublin: The Cuala Press,
    1929.
Wyndham Lewis. *Tarr*. London: Egoist Ltd., 1918.
BLAST. London: John Lane, 1914–15.

9

Wedding Announcement of Dorothy Shakespear to Ezra Pound.
    April 1914.
Ezra Pound. *Ripostes*. London: Stephen Swift, 1912.
Ezra Pound. *Canzoni & Ripostes*. London: Elkin Mathews, 1913.
Ezra Pound. *Lustra*. London: Elkin Mathews, 1916.

Joyce, Lawrence and Frost

Ezra Pound's efforts on behalf of other writers, particularly
in London in the teens, were tireless. Three writers whom
Pound promoted, recommended to editors, and reviewed
could not have been more different from one another:
David Herbert Lawrence, the son of a Nottinghamshire
miner; Robert Frost, who arrived in England in 1913 after
a period of farming in America; and James Joyce, an Irishman
whom Yeats thought had written some good lyric poetry.

Pound was never quite as sure-footed in his criticism about
prose as he was about poetry. "I can't usually read prose at all
not anybody's in English except James and Hudson and a little
Conrad. . . ," he wrote to Joyce upon reading the first chapter
of *A Portrait of the Artist as a Young Man*, and greatly preferred
Lawrence's poems to his novels. In his review of *Love Poems
and Others* (1913), he said of Lawrence, he "has brought
contemporary verse up to the level of contemporary prose."

Robert Frost was a writer whose work never had much appeal
to Pound, but Pound recognized the quality of Frost's "natural
speech," and promoted him and wrote a positive review of Frost's
first book, *A Boy's Will*, for *Poetry* magazine in 1913. Forty years

James Joyce.
Ulysses.
Paris: Shakespeare & Co.,
1922.

later, Frost's influence was instrumental in assisting with Pound's release from St. Elizabeths Hospital.

Pound first heard of James Joyce through Yeats, and contacted Joyce in Trieste in 1913. Joyce was at a low point; his book of poems *Chamber Music* had been published six years earlier and was his only book in print, and he was in poor financial straits trying to support his wife and two children. Joyce's difficulties in publishing his collection *Dubliners* were legendary; it took almost ten years for the volume to be published without expurgation. Pound was drawn by Joyce's travails with censorious publishers, and his support resulted in the publication of *A Portrait of the Artist as a Young Man* as a serialization in the *Egoist* in 1914. Joyce was extremely grateful to Pound for his support; he wrote to Yeats, "I can never thank you enough for having brought me into relation with your friend Ezra Pound who is indeed a miracle worker." It was several years later, in 1918, that Pound's machinations saw through the first serial publication of *Ulysses*, in *The Little Review*. Later, in Paris, Pound introduced Joyce to Sylvia Beach, the American bookseller and proprietor of Shakespeare and Company in Paris, who was to publish *Ulysses* in 1922. *Ulysses* stands, along with *The Waste Land*, as the pre-eminent modernist text, and the most influential novel of the twentieth century—an "impassioned meditation on life," as Pound wrote to Joyce.

———

D.H. Lawrence. *Love Poems and Others*. London: Duckworth, 1913.
D.H. Lawrence. *Amores*. London: Duckworth, 1916.
Robert Frost. *A Boy's Will*. London: David Nutt, 1913.
James Joyce. *Chamber Music*. London: Elkin Mathews, 1907.
James Joyce. *Dubliners*. London: Grant Richards, 1914.
James Joyce. *A Portrait of the Artist as a Young Man*. London:
    The Egoist Ltd., 1916.
James Joyce. *Ulysses*. Paris: Shakespeare and Company, 1922.

"A Heap of Broken Images": The Waste Land

Ezra Pound met T.S. Eliot in London in 1914, some time after he asked Conrad Aiken to recommend a poet who was doing modern, different work. Eliot was recently graduated from Harvard, doing post-graduate work in philosophy at Oxford University and

struggling with the conflicting ideas of becoming a professor
or dedicating himself to poetry. Pound read Eliot's "The Love
Song of J. Alfred Prufrock," immediately deeming it "the best
poem I have yet had or seen from an American," and took the
young poet under his wing. Harriet Monroe published "Prufrock"
in the June 1915 issue of *Poetry* on Pound's strenuous
recommendation, and several more Eliot poems later that year.
Pound included two poems of Eliot's in the second issue of
BLAST, published in July 1915. Eliot's first book, *Prufrock and
Other Observations*, was published in June 1917 by the Egoist
Press, although Pound had fronted the printing costs. *Poems*
was published by the Hogarth Press in 1919, followed the next
year by *Poems*, published by Alfred Knopf. Eliot also authored,
anonymously, a brief monograph on Pound's work which was
published by Knopf in 1917.

Eliot had secured a position in Lloyd's Bank in 1917, but the pay
was meager, even supplemented by Eliot's occasional reviews.
Pound had earlier attempted to raise funds so that Eliot could
leave the bank's employ to write full-time, but nothing came
of it; in 1922 Pound tried again with a plan called "Bel Esprit."
The printer John Rodker produced a printed missive, but Eliot's
innate uneasiness about the endeavor and other events
eventually caused its foundering.

The pressures of work and finances and Eliot's strained marriage
to Vivien Haigh-Wood culminated in a nervous breakdown.
He was ordered by a specialist to take a three-month leave of
absence from the bank; it was during his recuperation at Margate
and Lausanne in late 1921 that he applied himself in earnest to a
"sprawling chaotic poem" he had been considering for several

years. En route to Switzerland, he visited Pound in Paris in November and showed him the poem, originally entitled "He Do the Police in Different Voices" (Betty Higden's comment on the foundling Sloppy's oral reading of the newspaper in Dickens' *Our Mutual Friend*), but soon titled *The Waste Land*. Pound edited the poem substantially, deleting entire sections and calling for Eliot to tighten and rearrange others. The final product reflects almost as much Pound's vision of Eliot's poem as of Eliot's himself; Eliot's dedication of the poem to Pound as *il miglior fabbro* ("the better craftsman," and itself an allusion to Pound's work, as it was the phrase Dante had used to praise the troubadour poet Arnaut Daniel, whose work Pound had translated) reflected his thought that Pound had "done so much to turn *The Waste Land* from a jumble of good and bad passages into a poem."

The poem was published in October 1922 in the *Dial* (where it received the $2000 *Dial* Award, as payment for the poem due to intense negotiations by both Pound and Eliot with the *Dial* editors) and the *Criterion*, a new magazine edited by Eliot. It was published in book form in December by Boni & Liveright; this edition marked the first appearance of Eliot's notes to the poem. A later edition was published the following year by Leonard and Virginia Woolf at the Hogarth Press. The poem had great impact from the moment of its publication; the critic Lawrence Rainey has said, "the publication of *The Waste Land* marked the crucial moment in the transition of modernism from a minority culture to one supported by an important institutional and financial apparatus." It could be added that this was the vindication of everything Pound had been promoting for the past fifteen years, and marks the moment of his greatest triumph—the justification of "our modern experiment."

THE WASTE LAND

By ~~T. S. ELIOT~~ *T. S. Eliot*

I. THE BURIAL OF THE DEAD

APRIL is the cruellest month, breeding
Lilacs out of the dead land, mixing
Memory and desire, stirring
Dull roots with spring rain.
Winter kept us warm, covering
Earth in forgetful snow, feeding
A little life with dried tubers.
Summer surprised us, coming over the Starnbergersee
With a shower of rain ; we stopped in the colonnade,
And went on in the sunlight, into the Hofgarten,
And drank coffee, and talked for an hour.
Bin gar keine Russin, stamm' aus Litauen, echt deutsch.
And when we were children, staying at the archduke's,
My cousin's, he took me out on a sled,
And I was frightened.   He said, " Marie,
Marie, hold on tight."   And down we went.
In the mountains, there you feel free.
I read, much of the night, and go south in the winter.

What are the roots that clutch, what branches grow
Out of this stony rubbish ?   Son of man,
You cannot say, or guess, for you know only
A heap of broken images, where the sun beats,
And the dead tree gives no shelter, the cricket no relief,
And the dry stone no sound of water.   Only

First printed appearance of 'The Waste Land' in the *Criterion, A Quarterly Review.* v. 1, no. 1 (October 1922). p. 50.
Signed, with three corrections by Eliot.

The relationship between Pound and Eliot, although it continued primarily in correspondence, was never the same after 1922. Both wrote regular criticism of the other's work, and Eliot played a role in securing Pound's release from St. Elizabeths in 1958. Pound attended Eliot's memorial service in Westminster Abbey in 1965, and wrote of him, "His was the true Dantescan voice—not honoured enough, and deserving more than I ever gave him."

——

T.S. Eliot. *Ezra Pound: His Metric and Poetry*. New York: Alfred A. Knopf, 1917.

T.S. Eliot. *Poems*. Richmond: Printed & Pub. by L. & V. Woolf at the Hogarth Press, 1919.

The Criterion, A Quarterly Review. v. 1, no. 1 (Oct. 1922). London: R. Cobden-Sanderson. With autograph and three corrections by Eliot.

T.S. Eliot. *The Waste Land*. New York: Boni & Liveright, 1922.

T.S. Eliot. *The Waste Land*. Richmond: L. & V. Woolf, 1923.

Bel Esprit. [London: John Rodker, 1922.] Broadsheet.

T.S. Eliot. *The Waste Land*; A Facsimile and Transcript of the Original Drafts Including the Annotations of Ezra Pound. Edited by Valerie Eliot. New York: Harcourt Brace Jovanovich, [1971].

The Paris Years

Ezra Pound settled in Paris in 1921, and was to remain there for several years. He quickly met the nascent Surrealists (including Man Ray and Jean Cocteau), Gertrude Stein (neither Pound nor Stein were much impressed by the other), and a couple of young American writers, Ernest Hemingway and E.E. Cummings. He mingled at the salon of the American exile Natalie Barney, where he met some of the older French intellectuals, such as André Gide and Paul Valéry, and expatriate American writers such as Mina Loy. He continued his support of Joyce as *Ulysses* was eventually published in 1922, but their friendship cooled after Pound expressed his dislike for the first parts of "Work in Progress" (later *Finnegans Wake*). His first year in Paris also saw Pound working closely with T.S. Eliot on the poem that would soon be published as *The Waste Land*.

Ernest Hemingway met Pound late in 1921, and was soon teaching him how to box. Pound arranged for Hemingway's short prose vignettes to be published by William Bird and edited by Pound at Three Mountains Press as *in our time*. The book was issued in New York a year later in expanded form. *in our time* was noticed and reviewed, and Hemingway soon had a contract for his first novel, *The Sun Also Rises*, published in 1926.

The young E.E. Cummings was introduced to Pound in 1921, having published several poems in the *Dial*. Pound praised Cummings's work, calling it "bright inimitable," and Cummings later referred to Pound as "the true trailblazer of an epoch." Pound had met Marianne Moore in London in the previous decade, and recommended her work for publication in *Poetry* and *The Little Review*, but it was not until 1921 that her first book, *Poems*, was published. Pound included poems by Cummings and Moore in *Active Anthology*.

———

Marianne Moore. *Poems*. London: The Egoist Press, 1921.
Mina Loy. *Lunar Baedecker*. Paris: Contact Publishing Co., 1923.
Ernest Hemingway. *Three Stories & Ten Poems*. Paris: Contact
    Publishing Co., 1923.
Ernest Hemingway. *in our time*. Paris: Three Mountains Press, 1924.
Ernest Hemingway. *The Sun Also Rises*. New York: Scribner, 1926.
E.E. Cummings. *XLI Poems*. New York: Dial Press, 1925.
Jean Cocteau. *Opéra: Œuvres poétiques 1925–1927*. Paris: Stock, 1927.

Pound and Little Magazines

One of Pound's chief methods of disseminating information
and presenting the work of new poets was publication through
a variety of small literary and artistic-minded journals. His own
writings for these publications were often a financial lifeline as
well. In London, he wrote music and art reviews for *New Age*
under a pseudonym, and served as *Poetry* magazine's (self-
appointed) overseas editor (its founder, Harriet Monroe, had
contacted him in 1912 to see if he would contribute poems to
her new magazine), using the magazine to launch, among
others, Robert Frost, William Carlos Williams, T.S. Eliot,
and the Imagists, such as H.D. and Amy Lowell.

In 1917, Pound became the "foreign editor" of an American
magazine, *The Little Review*, which was founded in Chicago in
1914 by Margaret Anderson and joined in 1916 by Jane Heap. As
he stated, he wanted "a place where the current prose writings
of James Joyce, Wyndham Lewis, T.S. Eliot, and myself might
appear regularly, promptly, and together, rather than irregularly,
sporadically, and after useless delays." The magazine rapidly
became a showcase for Pound and his circle and serialized,
through Pound's urging, James Joyce's *Ulysses*, beginning
in 1918.

Pound also contributed to numerous other magazines during
this period, including the *Egoist* (where he placed Joyce's
Portrait of the Artist as a Young Man in 1916), the *Dial*, and
BLAST, which he co-edited with Wyndham Lewis. He fulfilled
a longstanding plan of running his own journal with the *Exile*,
which ran for four numbers in 1927 and 1928.

Pound was also involved with the journal *Pagany*, and
contributed material and advice to the editor, Richard Johns.
Johns had originally tried to have William Carlos Williams serve
as co-editor when the magazine was launched in 1929; Williams
declined, but he contributed his own work, solicited material
from others, and advised Johns on editorial matters.
———

The Little Review. (Chicago) Volume IV, no. 1, May 1917.
The Little Review. (Chicago) Volume V, no. 11, March 1918.
The Dial. (New York) Volume LXIX, no. 3, September 1920.
The Exile. Nos. 1–4. 1927–1928.
Ezra Pound to Richard Johns, editor of *Pagany*, autograph letter
    signed, November 3, 1930.

Pound as Anthologist

Over the course of his career, Pound compiled several book-
length poetry anthologies. These collections, as Pound's
publisher James Laughlin said, "enabled him to publicize
contemporary poets he liked and to establish critical values."
The first was *Des Imagistes*. Pound had several years earlier
created the idea of "Imagism" and promptly recruited several
friends into the fold, such as Hilda Doolittle and her husband
Richard Aldington. The poet F.S. Flint wrote a manifesto, as
demonstrated and edited by Pound, about them which was
published in the March 1913 issue of *Poetry*. Pound's anthology,
published the following year, included work by H.D., Aldington,
Flint, James Joyce, Williams, and Pound himself.

The next year, 1915, saw the publication of *Catholic Anthology*,
which Pound had compiled for the express reason of printing

T.S. Eliot's verse, notably "The Love Song of J. Alfred Prufrock."
Pound also included work by Yeats, William Carlos Williams,
Edgar Lee Masters, and Carl Sandburg. *Profile* was published in
1932 by the Milanese publisher Giovanni Scheiwiller. Pound
referred to it as a "collection of poems which have stayed in my
memory;" it included poems by Eliot, Bunting, Hemingway,
Mina Loy, Arthur Symons, and many others.

Active Anthology was published by Faber & Faber in England the
following year; its stated intent was to introduce new poets, such
as Louis Zukofsky and George Oppen. Pound also included work
by E.E. Cummings, Marianne Moore, and T.S. Eliot, among others.

Although not an anthology per se, Pound's *ABC of Reading* was
an enormously influential work of pedagogy; as noted by James
Laughlin, Pound "uses his anthological method to show the
poetry which makes up his 'canon'."

In 1964, New Directions published an anthology that Pound had
assembled along with Marcella Spann, a young teacher who
had visited Pound at St. Elizabeths Hospital. Titled *Confucius
to Cummings*, the anthology was intended for classroom use
and contains a "section for instructors" at the end. As the title
indicates, it contains poems ranging from the ancient world
to Yeats, Eliot, and Cummings.

———

Ezra Pound, ed. *Des Imagistes*. New York: Boni, 1914.
Ezra Pound, ed. *Catholic Anthology*. London: Elkin Mathews, 1915.
Ezra Pound, ed. *Profile*. Milan: Scheiwiller, 1932.
Ezra Pound, ed. *Active Anthology*. London: Faber & Faber, 1933.
Ezra Pound. *ABC of Reading*. London: George Routledge and Sons, 1934.
Ezra Pound and Marcella Spann, ed. *Confucius to Cummings: An
Anthology of Poetry*. New York: New Directions, 1964.

Catholic Anthology 1914–1915. London: Elkin Mathews, 1915.
Cover design by Dorothy Shakespear Pound.

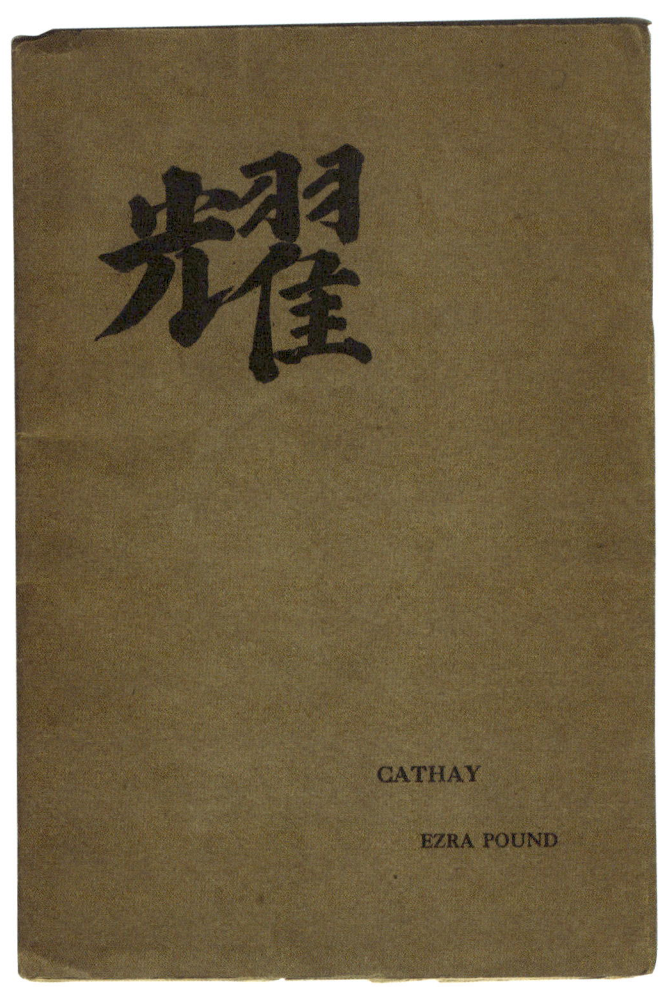

Ezra Pound. *Cathay*.

Pound and Translation

In 1913, Pound was given several notebooks of writings and
translations by the late sinologist Ernest Fenollosa. The work
he did on this material proved to be a watershed not only in his
own translating projects but set a course for modern poetry; as
Eliot later noted, "each generation must translate for itself."
Pound's versions of Fenollosa's Chinese poems, published as
Cathay in 1915, "altered the feel of the language and set the
pattern of cadence for modern verse," as George Steiner has
said. Chinese was to inform Pound's translations and writing
for the rest of his career, from the many passages in the *Cantos*
to his work on *The Classic Anthology as Defined by Confucius*.
His stewardship of Fenollosa's essay "The Chinese Written
Character as a Medium for Poetry" also proved extremely
influential.

Pound was immersed in his early school years in the study of
languages, and one of his first published works of prose was
The Spirit of Romance (1910), a study of medieval literature,
which contained some of his first attempts at translations of the
lyrics of the troubadours. He continued to study and work on
troubadour lyrics for years, and also the works of Dante's
contemporary, Guido Cavalcanti.

Hugh Kenner wrote in *The Pound Era* that Pound "came to
think of translation as a model for the poetic act: blood brought
to ghosts." Kenner later notes, "translation . . . after Ezra Pound,
aims neither at dim ritual nor at lexicographic lockstep, but at
seeming transparency, the vigors of the great original . . . not
remote but at touching distance, though only to be touched with
the help of all that we know."

Ezra Pound. *The Spirit of Romance*. London: J.M. Dent, 1910.

Ezra Pound. *The Sonnets and Ballate of Guido Cavalcanti*. Boston: Small, Maynard, 1912.

Ezra Pound. *Cathay*. London: Elkin Mathews, 1915.

Ezra Pound. *Certain Noble Plays of Japan*. Churchtown Dundrum: The Cuala Press, 1916.

Ernest Fenollosa. *The Chinese Written Character as a Medium for Poetry*. London: Stanley Nott, 1936.

Ezra Pound. *The Classic Anthology as Defined by Confucius*. Cambridge: Harvard University Press, 1954. Galley proofs, with corrections by Pound.

Pound and the Objectivists

Ezra Pound's short-lived journal the *Exile*, which ran for four issues in 1927 and 1928, published a poem by the young New York poet Louis Zukofsky. Zukofsky was a great admirer of Pound's and looked to him as a mentor. He established a group of poets called the Objectivists, whose mission Zukofsky described as "desire for what is objectively perfect, inextricably the direction of historic and contemporary particulars." Other members of the group included William Carlos Williams (whose *Collected Poems 1921–1931* was published by the Objectivist Press), Basil Bunting, and George Oppen, who financed the Press. Pound included all of these poets, along with Cummings, Eliot, Marianne Moore, and others, in his *Active Anthology* of 1933. Zukofsky's epic poem *"A"* is considered, alongside the *Cantos* and *Paterson*, as one of the more indefinable and unique products of twentieth-century poetry.

———

Basil Bunting. *Redimiculum matellarum*. Milan: [s.n.], 1930. (*Milano: Stampato nelle Officine de la Grafica Moderna*)

Louis Zukofsky, ed. *An "Objectivists" Anthology*. Le Beausset, France;
    New York: To, Publishers, 1932.
George Oppen. *Discrete Series*. New York: Objectivist Press, 1934.
William Carlos Williams. *Collected Poems 1921–1931*. New York:
    Objectivist Press, 1934.
Louis Zukofsky. *First Half of "A"-9*. New York: [The Author], 1940.
Louis Zukofsky. *55 Poems*. Prairie City, Illinois: Press of James A. Decker,
    1941.

Pound and Laughlin

In 1933, Pound received a letter from a young Harvard student
named James Laughlin IV, requesting permission to visit him
in Rapallo, Italy, where Pound was then living. Laughlin spent
some time with Pound, learning and soaking in the artistic
milieu, listening to Pound's discourse on literature, history,
languages, and the news of the day. Laughlin was an aspiring
poet, but Pound was dismissive of his work, telling him to go
back to America "and do something useful." When Laughlin
asked what might be useful, Pound suggested, "go back and be
a publisher."

With the help of family money, Laughlin took Pound's advice to
heart, and his first publication was an anthology, *New Directions
in Prose and Poetry*, published in 1936. Included in the anthology
were Pound's "Canto 44," along with works by Elizabeth Bishop,
William Carlos Williams, Gertrude Stein, E.E. Cummings,
Marianne Moore, and others. The first book of Pound's
published under the New Directions imprint was *Culture*,
which appeared in 1938. New Directions became a constant in
Pound's career; Laughlin kept all of his books in print. He also
published challenging new work by William Carlos Williams,

Kenneth Rexroth, Dylan Thomas, and Henry Miller, and later
the Beats and other poets. New Directions remains a formidable
publishing house and publishes poetry, modern literature, and
literature in translation, staying true to the ethos of its founder,
Laughlin,who died in 1997.

———

Ezra Pound. *Culture.* Norfolk: New Directions, 1938.

Ezra Pound at Seventy. Norfolk: New Directions, 1955.

James Laughlin. *Gists & Piths.* Iowa City: Windhover Press, 1982. This is
one of 25 copies, signed by Laughlin, with a postcard from Pound to
Laughlin laid in.

James Laughlin. *Ezra.* New York: Dim Gray Bar Press, 1994. One of one
hundred copies, with photographs by Laughlin.

James Laughlin. *Byways.* New York: New Directions, 2004.

"An Endless Poem of No Known Category": The Cantos

In September 1915, Pound wrote to a correspondent that he was
"at work on a cryselephantine poem of immeasurable length
which will occupy me for the next four decades unless it becomes
a bore." Greatly influenced by Browning's *Sordello* at first, the
Cantos ultimately became his life's work, published in various
installments, over the next fifty years, as he predicted. Much
has been written about the *Cantos*; suffice it to say that they
stand as a monument of twentieth-century literature, alongside
The Waste Land, Paterson, The Maximus Poems and *"A"* (all of
which Pound directly influenced) as an epic poem which will still
be explicated and deciphered well into the twenty-first century.

———

Ezra Pound. *A Draft of XVI Cantos of Ezra Pound: For the Beginning of a
Poem of Some Length.* Paris: Three Mountains Press, 1925. One of
90 copies.

Ezra Pound. *A Draft of the Cantos 17–27 of Ezra Pound*. London: John Rodker, 1928.

Ezra Pound. *A Draft of XXX Cantos*. Paris: Hours Press, 1930. This copy is inscribed by Pound.

Ezra Pound. *Eleven New Cantos XXXI–XLI*. New York: Farrar & Rinehart, 1934.

Ezra Pound. *The Fifth Decad of Cantos*. New York: Farrar & Rinehart, 1937.

Ezra Pound. *Cantos LII–LXXI*. Norfolk: New Directions, 1940.

Ezra Pound. *Section, Rock-Drill: 85–95 de los Cantares*. New York: New Directions, 1957.

Ezra Pound. *Thrones: 96–109 de los Cantares*. New York: New Directions, 1959.

Ezra Pound. *Drafts & Fragments of Cantos CX–CVIII*. New York: New Directions, 1968.

The Cantos of Ezra Pound: Some Testimonies. New York: Farrar & Rinehart, 1933. Contributions by Edmund Wilson, William Carlos Williams, H.D., Allen Tate, James Joyce, Ford Madox Ford, T.S. Eliot, Basil Bunting, and John Peale Bishop.

World War II, The Pisan Cantos and St. Elizabeths

Through the late 1920s and 1930s, Pound became more and more interested in politics and economics. Typically, he began writing tracts and treatises about these subjects. Living in Italy, he embraced the fascist government of Benito Mussolini, writing a book titled *Jefferson and/or Mussolini* (1935), and became more vocal in his support of Italian fascism and anti-Americanism. In January 1941, he made the first of his Italian radio broadcasts, warning against U.S. involvement in the war. He would continue to be broadcast until the fall of the Fascist government in July 1943. Adopting elements of the speeches of American demagogue radio commentator Father Charles Coughlin, Pound's vituperative broadcasts were characterized by anti-Semitic invective and

attacks on Roosevelt and Churchill, along with other topics of
interest to Pound, such as Confucius. These radio broadcasts
were monitored by the United States Federal Broadcast
Intelligence Service. In 1945, following Germany's defeat in
Italy, Pound was arrested by partisans and released. He turned
himself in to the American forces and was transferred to a U.S.
Army prison camp in Pisa. Pound, then almost sixty, was held in
solitary confinement in a reinforced steel cage. After three weeks
he suffered a mental breakdown and was transferred to a tent;
here he began composing *The Pisan Cantos*. Pound was flown
to Washington, D.C., in November and charged with treason.
After a psychiatric examination, he was found mentally unfit
for trial and "suffering from a paranoid state," and was sent to
St. Elizabeths Hospital in Washington.

Pound would spend the next thirteen years there. As the poet,
critic, and Pound acolyte Guy Davenport has written, Pound,
once "known in literary circles as . . . an erudite poet of awesome
difficulty, was suddenly famous as a crazy, anti-Semitic Fascist."
The critic F.R. Leavis noted that "the spectacle of Pound's
degeneration is a terrible one and no one ought to pretend that
it is anything but what it is." After *The Pisan Cantos* were
published by New Directions in 1948, the Fellows in American
Literature at the Library of Congress chose to award the book
the first annual Bollingen Prize. Public outcry followed, including
several attacks by Robert Hillyer in the *Saturday Review of
Literature*, but the committee, anticipating controversy, held
firm. In the hospital, Pound continued to work on his Confucian
translations and *Cantos*, and was visited by a steady stream
of friends and disciples, including such younger poets as
Robert Lowell (who had begun correspondence with Pound
while still a Harvard student), Robert Duncan, Randall Jarrell,

and Elizabeth Bishop, who wrote a poem called "Visits to
St. Elizabeths," published in *Questions of Travel*. Following
years of appeals and petitions, Pound was released from the
hospital in 1958, his treason indictment dismissed on the
grounds that he would never be fit for trial. Many of his old
friends and those he had supported in the early years rallied to
his cause, including Archibald MacLeish, Eliot, Hemingway,
and crucially Robert Frost, who by that point had some political
influence and personally lobbied members of the Eisenhower
administration on Pound's behalf.

Following his release, Pound returned to Italy, where he divided
the rest of his time between Rapallo and Venice, working
intermittently on the Cantos and retreating into silence and
depression. He died in Venice on November 1, 1972, the day after
his eighty-seventh birthday.

———

Ezra Pound. *ABC of Economics*. London: Faber & Faber, 1933.
    Louis Zukofsky's copy, with his inscription dated 1933.
Ezra Pound. *Jefferson and/or Mussolini*. London: Stanley Nott, 1935.
Ezra Pound. *If This be Treason*. Siena: Printed for Olga Rudge by Tip.
    Nuova, 1948.
Harold H. Watts. *Ezra Pound and the Cantos*. Chicago: Henry Regnery
    Company, 1952. This copy is from the Circulating Library of
    St. Elizabeths Hospital.
Ezra Pound. *The Pisan Cantos*. New York: New Directions, 1948.
    Louis Zukofsky's copy, with his inscription dated 1948.
Open Letter to the Editors, *Saturday Review of Literature*, 1949.
    Broadsheet letter.
Charles Norman. *The Case of Ezra Pound*. New York: The Bodley Press,
    1948.
Elizabeth Bishop. *Questions of Travel*. New York: Farrar Straus Giroux,
    1965.

After Pound

Pound cast a long shadow over literary modernism, beginning
with those writers he directly supported and promoted, and
he continued to exert an influence over younger writers well
into the second half of the twentieth century. Charles Olson
was one of Pound's first visitors to St. Elizabeths; a committed
anti-fascist, he later drifted from Pound's circle but never
renounced his debt to the older writer as a mentor. His *Maximus
Poems* are a *Cantos*-like kaleidoscope of poetry. Robert Creeley
and Robert Duncan both corresponded with Pound while he was
in the hospital; the Black Mountain School of poetry, with which
Creeley, Duncan and Denise Levertov were all associated, took
Pound's modernism a step further. Duncan served as secretary
to H.D. in her later years, and Creeley was close with Zukofsky
and William Carlos Williams. Allen Ginsberg visited Pound in
Venice in 1967—it was to Ginsberg that Pound reportedly said,
"the worst mistake I made was that stupid, suburban prejudice
of anti-Semitism." Furthering the connection between the
generations, William Carlos Williams wrote the introduction
to Ginsberg's seminal poem *Howl*. The elusive American poet
Jack Gilbert visited Pound in Merano in 1960. When Gilbert
asked if Pound thought that younger poets would continue in
the high modernist tradition of Pound's *Cantos*, Pound, after
twenty minutes' silence, said, "No, what I have done for the
young poets is to make it possible for them to put things in
their poems."

Pound's legacy was further advanced in the works of poets
such as Lorine Niedecker, Paul Blackburn (whose translations
of troubadour poets were directly influenced by Pound's earlier
work on the same writers) and Guy Davenport, the Language

Poets, such as Charles Bernstein and Jackson Mac Low, the oblique and musical ruminations of John Ashbery, and the narrative rhythms of Charles Wright. Pound's famous dictum to "make it new," the movement he created and the works he championed, still resonate in modern literature.

———

Lorine Niedecker. *New Goose*. Prairie City, Illinois: Press of James A. Decker, 1946.

Robert Creeley. *Le Fou*. Columbus: Golden Goose Press, 1952.

Paul Blackburn. *Proensa: from the Provençal of Guillem de Peitau, Arnaut de Marueill, Raimbautz de Vaqueiras, Sordello, Bernart de Ventadorn, Peire Vidal, Bertran de Born*. Palma de Mallorca: Divers Press, 1953.

Allen Ginsberg. *Howl*. San Francisco: City Lights Books, 1955.

Denise Levertov. *Overland to the Islands*. Highlands: J. Williams, 1958.

Charles Olson. *The Maximus Poems*. New York: Jargon/Corinth Books, 1960.

Robert Duncan. *The Opening of the Field*. New York: Evergreen Books, 1960.

Guy Davenport. *Thasos and Ohio: Poems and Translations 1950–1980*. San Francisco: North Point Press, 1986.

Envoi

I have tried to write Paradise

Do not move
    Let the wind speak
        that is paradise.

Let the Gods forgive what I
        have made
Let those I love try to forgive
        what I have made.

from *Notes for Canto CXVII*

Robert A.Wilson seated in front of his Ezra Pound collection.

About Robert A. Wilson

Robert A. Wilson was born in Baltimore in 1922. After graduating from Johns Hopkins University in 1943 he entered the U.S. Army and served in Germany. Following his discharge from the Army, he joined the United States Diplomatic Corps and held positions in various countries, including as Third Secretary of the Embassy in Warsaw, Poland and Pretoria, South Africa. He left the Diplomatic Corps and moved to New York and eventually entered the profession of antiquarian bookselling. In 1962, he became the fifth owner of the Phoenix Book Shop in Greenwich Village.

Under Robert Wilson's management, the Phoenix was transformed from a small bookshop on an obscure street in Greenwich Village into a legendary literary haven which became one of the most important bookstores of the era. During his ownership Robert Wilson bought and sold the books and manuscripts of a wide range of American, British, and other authors. The Phoenix also became a destination of choice for collectors, scholars, and authors, and Robert Wilson met and befriended many of the most prominent contemporary authors and artists of the period. He operated the Phoenix Book Shop until 1988 when he sold the business and moved to St. Michaels, Maryland, where he currently resides.

In addition to his successful career as a bookseller, Robert Wilson is also an author of note. He is the bibliographer of Gertrude Stein, Gregory Corso and Denise Levertov, and the author of a number of books, including *Modern Book Collecting* (1980) and the autobiographical *Seeing Shelley Plain* (2001).

Wilson and the Phoenix Book Shop are also celebrated in the
collection *The Phoenix Book Shop: a Nest of Memories* (1997),
which includes short essays and tributes from such authors as
Amiri Baraka, John Ashbery, Marshall Clements, Diane di Prima,
Allen Ginsberg, James Purdy, Ed Sanders, Michael McClure,
and others.

Robert Wilson has also been a book collector for his entire life
and assembled magnificent collections of the work of these and
other authors, a number of which are housed in the Special
Collections of the University of Delaware Library. A significant
portion have been gifts from this generous collector.

In "Ezra Pound in His Time and Beyond," the University of
Delaware Library highlights one of his most comprehensive
collections and pays tribute to Robert A.Wilson, bookseller,
bibliographer, and collector extraordinaire.

Membership Information about the University of Delaware Library Associates

Founded in 1958, the University of Delaware Library Associates works to enrich the research collections of the University of Delaware Library through gifts from individual members, funds raised by University of Delaware Library Associates programs, and donations of significant books.

The University of Delaware Library Associates also sponsors publications and other activities that make the collections better known to the University of Delaware, to the national scholarly communities, and to the members of the general public.

Membership in the University of Delaware Library Associates is actively solicited. Contributions are tax deductible to the fullest extent of the law. For further information or to request a membership brochure about the University of Delaware Library Associates, one can contact:

> University of Delaware Library Associates
> Morris Library
> University of Delaware
> Newark, DE 19717-5267
> 302-831 2231 phone
> 302-831-1046 fax
> udla@udel.edu

The membership brochure may be found on the University of Delaware Library website at http://www.lib.udel.edu. Select "Information," then select "Friends and Donors."

The University of Delaware Library exhibitions are also available via the Library Web by selecting "Services," then select "Special Collections."